# Dinosaurs

Written by Dan Abnett and Nik Vincent

**DP**
DEMPSEY
PARR

This edition is for Books Are Fun

This is a Dempsey Parr Book
First published in 2000

Dempsey Parr is an imprint of Parragon
Parragon
Queen Street House
4 Queen Street
Bath BA1 1HE, UK

ISBN 1-84084-777-8

Printed in Dubai, U.A.E

Designer: Matt Neal
Editor: Audrey Daly

# Contents

# How did dinosaurs evolve?

Dinosaurs first lived on Earth 230 million years ago. They evolved from reptiles, which were the first animals to live out of water all the time. All creatures before the reptiles could only live in water, or partly in water and partly on land. Reptiles lived in the Triassic period, and were like lizards with legs on the sides of their bodies. Then, over the centuries, their legs began to grow beneath their bodies, so that they could walk upright some of the time — and so, dinosaurs began to evolve.

The first animals to walk upright were called Thecodonts. They were the ancestors of the first dinosaurs. Walking upright meant that the dinosaurs could see more of what was around them, and they could run faster.

### What kinds of animals did dinosaurs evolve from?

They evolved from the Thecodont, a type of archosaur that could walk upright some of the time. The Thecodonts were reptiles, and looked a little like modern crocodiles. The Thecodonts, unlike other reptiles at that time, had legs underneath their bodies instead of at the sides.

### What was an archosaur like?

Archosaur means "ruling lizard," so named because this group of reptiles was more advanced than others of its time.

To help them to swim, archosaurs had developed strong hind legs and long, strong tails. When they took to the land, this meant they could walk on their hind legs, balanced by their tails. Their short front legs had claws to catch animals, and they had sharp teeth to cut meat.

### Did all the reptiles change?

One group of reptiles evolved into dinosaurs, but there were many other kinds of reptiles around at the time. Some reptiles returned to the water and some developed into other land animals, including mammals. There are still as many as 6,500 different kinds of reptiles living on Earth today, some looking very much like those of dinosaur times.

The name reptile comes from the Latin word meaning "to crawl."

The Mesosaur was an early reptile.

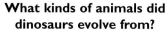

# Did all archosaurs evolve into dinosaurs?

**A**LTHOUGH THE GROUP OF ARCHOSAURS CALLED THECODONTS DEVELOPED INTO dinosaurs, other archosaurs evolved into different kinds of animals or died out. Some archosaurs became pterosaurs—flying reptiles—and some developed into the crocodiles of today.

### How long did it take for reptiles to evolve into dinosaurs?

Evolution is a long and slow process. The first reptiles appeared during the Carboniferous period, around 340 million years ago. The first dinosaurs appeared around 100 million years later; there were a number of different types of creatures between the two time periods.

### How long did the dinosaurs inhabit Earth?

The dinosaurs lived on Earth for about 165 million years. They lived all over the globe, adapting the way they lived to suit different habitats.

Lycaenops was a ferocious reptile that developed about the same time as the dinosaurs.

### How many different kinds of dinosaurs were there?

No one knows just how many different kinds of dinosaurs there were. Some dinosaurs evolved and some became extinct, so dinosaurs changed over the millions of years they were on Earth. Scientists are still finding examples of new dinosaurs all the time, so we may never know how many types there actually were.

### Where did the name dinosaur come from?

Two hundred years ago, people knew very little about dinosaurs. The word dinosaur means "terrible lizard." However, it is now known that dinosaurs were only very distantly related to lizards. And many of them were herbivores (plant-eating), so they did not fight or hunt for food.

### How long have we known about dinosaurs?

The first dinosaur bones were found hundreds of years ago, but nobody knew what they were. Then, about two hundred years ago, scientists began to take an interest in these strange finds, trying to figure out what they might be.

**How were the dinosaurs different from the Thecodonts?**

The Thecodonts developed from amphibians that lived in and out of water and could walk upright some of the time. The Thecodonts didn't evolve into dinosaurs until they could walk upright all the time, giving them a better field of vision and other uses for their front legs.

**Did early dinosaurs live near the water?**

Dinosaurs developed from reptiles, which were the first animals that didn't need to live near water. And they were the first creatures that could lay their eggs on land instead of in the water. Dinosaurs did not need to live near water, which meant they could move all over the landmass of the Earth.

# What did the first dinosaurs look like?

DINOSAURS REMIND US OF MODERN REPTILES SUCH AS CROCODILES.

For millions of years, dinosaurs were the most successful animals on Earth, because they could adapt to almost any condition. Some were meat-eating and some were plant-eating, and they came in all shapes and sizes, from the tiny Compsognathus to the huge Ultrasaurus at 100 feet long.

Ultrasaurus and Apatosaurus were both large plant-eating dinosaurs.

### Did all dinosaurs walk upright?

The earliest dinosaurs, like the Staurikosaurus and the Herrerasaurus, could walk upright, but other plant-eating dinosaurs that developed walked on four legs. They had small heads but long necks, so they were still tall enough to be able to see around them.

### When did the archosaurs live?

The archosaurs appeared about halfway through the Triassic period (which was between 213 and 248 million years ago).
The very earliest dinosaurs evolved later in the same period.

### When did the first dinosaurs appear on Earth?

The first dinosaur, Staurikosaurus, appeared about 225 or 230 million years ago, toward the end of the Triassic period, and survived for about five million years.

### What were the advantages of walking upright to a dinosaur?

Reptiles before the dinosaurs could not walk upright on their back legs. This meant that they were fairly slow and could not see very much above ground level. Dinosaurs' back legs were strong, so they could run faster. They could also use their front legs for gathering or hunting, or even, sometimes, for fighting.

# Are there any modern animals that evolved at the same time as dinosaurs?

SOME OF OUR MODERN REPTILES LOOK LIKE DINOSAURS, AND SOME TYPES OF TURTLES began to appear at about the same time. They have changed very little in millions of years, and look just as they did in the Triassic period.

At 36 feet long, Allosaurus was one of the largest meat-eaters.

Lizard-hipped
dinosaurs included
the Tyrannosaurus.

**When did the two types
of dinosaur appear?**
They appeared on Earth at about
the same time, although the earliest
known dinosaur, the Staurikosaurus,
was a lizard-hipped Saurischian.
The bird-hipped dinosaurs are
almost as old as the oldest
lizard-hipped dinosaurs.

Bird-hipped dinosaurs
included the Stegosaurus.

**Were all the
dinosaurs related?**
All dinosaurs appear to have
evolved from the Thecodonts.
Some scientists however, think that
they must have developed from
slightly different creatures, since
some have lizard hips and some
have bird hips.

# What were the two types of dinosaurs?

THERE WERE TWO MAIN TYPES OF
DINOSAURS. THE MOST IMPORTANT
difference between the two is in the shape of their hip
joints. Dinosaurs with pelvic or hipbones like lizards are
called Saurischia. This group includes both meat-eating
dinosaurs and the huge four-legged plant-eating
dinosaurs. Dinosaurs in the second group are called
Ornithischia, and are those with pelvic or hipbones more
like birds. All bird-hipped dinosaurs were plant-eating, and
were smaller than the plant-eating sauropods.

**Were there groups of
dinosaurs within these two
main groups?**
The Saurischian dinosaurs can be
divided into two groups. The
theropods walked upright and were
meat-eaters. The sauropods were
plant-eaters and walked on four
legs. They had long necks, and
most of them were gigantic.
The Ornisthician dinosaurs were all
plant-eaters, but could also be
divided into two groups.
The fabrosaurs had non-grinding
teeth, and the heterodontosaurs
had grinding teeth.

The Heterodontosaurus was one
of the earliest bird-hipped dinosaurs.

**Why did the plant-eating sauropods walk on four legs?**

Many sauropods were meat-eaters and walked on two legs, but large plant-eating dinosaurs needed bigger stomachs. Meat is rich in nutrients, but plant-eating dinosaurs had to eat a lot more to get the same amount of nutrients from their food.

The plant-eating sauropods had bigger stomachs so they couldn't balance properly on two legs. They had to walk on four legs.

**How big were the dinosaurs?**

One of the largest known dinosaurs was the lizard-hipped Ultrasaurus, which ate plants. It was 100 feet long and, with its long neck, it stood taller than a modern three-story house. Some of the smaller dinosaurs such as the Compsognathus were less than three feet long.

**Was one type of dinosaur more successful than the other?**

Both the Saurischia and the Ornisthicia evolved and changed throughout the age of the dinosaurs, but they both continued in their different forms until the dinosaurs became extinct. There is no evidence to suggest that one group took over or was more successful than the other.

The Compsognathus was only about 28 inches long. It ate insects and lizards.

The Mamenchisaurus was another large plant-eating sauropod.

# Were there any other differences between the two types of dinosaurs?

ALTHOUGH THE MOST OBVIOUS DIFFERENCE IS THE SHAPE OF THEIR pelvic or hipbones, there are other differences. The bird-hipped dinosaurs have a bone at the end of their lower jaw, but the lizard-hipped dinosaurs don't have this. The two types also have different kinds of teeth. Bird-hips have strengthened backbones, too, which look different from those of lizard-hipped ones.

No evidence has been found to show that one type of dinosaur evolved from the other and, because of the differences between them, scientists believe they evolved from different kinds of creatures.

# What was the Triassic period?

THE TRIASSIC PERIOD WAS A TIME IN EARTH'S HISTORY BETWEEN 248 AND 213 million years ago. Earth looked very different then. All the land of the world was joined together in one piece, not separated by seas and oceans as it is today. The landmass of the Triassic period is called the Pangaea.

The land was different because there were no grasses or flowers.

The plants were mostly conifers, like fir trees, and ferns of all kinds. The weather was also much drier than it is now.

Earth looked very different (1) 200 million years (2) 100 million years ago from how it looks today (3).

**What does Triassic mean?**
Scientists have given the name Triassic (from trias, meaning three) to the three-layered rock system in which the remains of the first dinosaurs have been found. The Triassic period was followed by the Jurassic period.

**What were the first dinosaurs?**
Two of the very earliest dinosaurs were small meat-eaters. The Herrerasaurus and the Staurikosaurus were only seven to ten feet long and walked upright.

Little is known about these Saurischians, but the Staurikosaurus had long back legs and probably moved fairly quickly.

The Herrerasaurus was heavier, with a large head and strong jaws.

Two of the earliest dinosaurs were Herrerasaurus and Staurikosaurus.

### Where did the first dinosaurs live?

Although the earliest dinosaur remains were found in South America, this does not mean that the first dinosaurs came from there. During the Triassic period, South America was joined to Africa.

The Pteranodon is one example of a pterosaur.

### Where else in the world have early dinosaurs been found?

Many early dinosaurs have been found all over the world in North America, South Africa, Europe and China, although the earliest were found in Brazil.

### Were there other kinds of dinosaurs at this time?

Very few fossils exist from the time of the first dinosaurs. However, there is evidence that there were other creatures that were evolving into dinosaurs at this time.

# What other kinds of animals existed in the Triassic period?

DURING THE TRIASSIC PERIOD, WHEN THE DINOSAURS FIRST APPEARED, THERE WERE all kinds of creatures both on land and in the water. The earliest mammals, warm-blooded creatures with hair or fur, appeared at about the same time as dinosaurs. Dinosaurs were stronger and better adapted to conditions, however, so many of the earliest mammals soon died out. But after the dinosaurs themselves became extinct, mammals took over as the most successful animals on Earth.

### Were there animals in the water?

Many water creatures continued to thrive in the seas and oceans of Earth, including reptiles that lived partly on the land. Eventually, these sorts of reptiles died out. However, the smaller crocodiles and turtles still exist today.

### Were there any birds?

The first flying animals appeared over 200 million years ago. They were more like flying reptiles than birds, and were called pterosaurs. The pterosaurs ruled the skies while the dinosaurs ruled the land.

**What does Jurassic mean?**

The Jurassic period is recognized by layers of rock in the ground at a different level from the Triassic. These layers are made of the same type of rock as the Jura mountains, and that is how they got the name Jurassic.

# What was the Jurassic period?

THE JURASSIC PERIOD WAS A TIME IN EARTH'S HISTORY BETWEEN 213 AND 144 million years ago. It is probably the most famous period of dinosaur history, because it was then that dinosaurs became the dominant land animals. The continents of Earth were still very close together, so the dinosaurs were able to roam and spread all over the world. This was the time of the really huge dinosaurs like the Ultrasaurus.

The Megalosaurus or "great lizard" was a meat-eating dinosaur found in the UK. It was 30 feet long.

**How had the dinosaurs developed?**

Since dinosaurs didn't have other animals to compete with, they were able to develop and adapt to the climate and landscape of Earth unhindered. They became the most successful of the land animals. There was an abundance of food for the plant-eating dinosaurs, which meant that there were plenty of plant-eating dinosaurs to provide meat for the larger meat-eating dinosaurs.

**How did dinosaurs evolve to cope with their size?**

The largest dinosaurs were the biggest land animals ever seen on Earth, and to accommodate their huge size they had to evolve in certain ways. One way was that their skeletons had to become very strong to support their huge bulk.

**How was Earth changing?**

By the end of the Jurassic period, the landmass known as the Pangaea had begun to split up and separate into continents. But land bridges between these new continents meant that the dinosaurs could still move wherever they wanted to. There was more rain at this time and plants were plentiful. As the Jurassic period was ending, the first flowering plants had started to appear.

## How large were the dinosaurs from the Jurassic period?

Diplodocus was an 88-foot-long plant-eating dinosaur and Allosaurus was a 35-foot-long meat-eater, but the biggest of the plant-eaters was the Brachiosaurus, and the biggest meat-eater was Megalosaurus Ingens.

## What other animals existed during the Jurassic period?

The only animals on Earth at this time that were more than three feet long were all dinosaurs. There were also tiny mammals and of course insects, but Earth was certainly dominated by dinosaurs of all kinds. Surprisingly, no dinosaurs ever learned to live in the seas and oceans of the world, nor did they learn to fly. They were very well adapted to the land and never ventured from it.

The Archaeopteryx — the very first bird.

## Were the sea creatures changing?

The seas swarmed with fish of all kinds, which were beginning to look more and more like the fish we know today. There were also ammonites, which are now extinct. Meat-eating reptiles called ichthyosaurs and plesiosaurs still inhabited the seas, preying on the fish.

# Were there any birds?

THE SKIES HAD BEEN CONTROLLED BY THE FLYING REPTILES CALLED PTEROSAURS UNTIL the first birds began to appear at the end of the Jurassic period. The first known bird is called Archaeopteryx. It was a long time, however, before the pterosaurs became extinct and modern birds took over.

The Shonisaurus was the largest ichthyosaur. It was 50 feet long.

**What does Cretaceous mean?**
The Cretaceous period was named after the chalk layers where dinosaur remains from this time are found. Cretaceous simply means "chalky."

The Tyrannosaurus was one of the last new dinosaurs.

# What was the Cretaceous period?

THE CRETACEOUS PERIOD WAS A TIME IN EARTH'S HISTORY FROM 144 TO 65 MILLION years ago. It was the last period in which there were dinosaurs on Earth. By the end of this time they were extinct. Chalk beds were forming on Earth then, and this age is named after them.

**Which dinosaurs did well during the Cretaceous period?**
The successful stegosaurs and sauropods were common dinosaurs during the Jurassic period, but began to die out and become isolated during the Cretaceous. Ankylosaurs had been around during the Jurassic period, and flourished during the Cretaceous. This suggests that they were better able to cope with the changes in the Earth at this time. The mighty Tyrannosaurs also did well then, living in Asia and North America.

**How was the Earth changing?**
Earth continued to change. The landmasses were moving further and further apart, becoming islands with seas around them. Plants also began to change — there were more and more flowering plants that couldn't grow all year round. The Earth began to have seasons, which meant colder winters and warmer summers.

**How did the changing world affect the dinosaurs?**
Changes in the landmass of the Earth meant that the dinosaurs became trapped between the seas and couldn't move around so easily. The changes in plants meant a lack of food for the plant-eating dinosaurs, and the new seasons meant that dinosaurs had to adapt to heat and cold in order to survive. All these changes may be why the dinosaurs began to die out.

**Did some Cretaceous dinosaurs flourish throughout the world?**
The Iguanodons also did well during this period, and their fossils have been found all over the world. It is unusual for the later dinosaurs to be so widespread because the landmass of Earth was breaking up and seas and oceans were separating the continents. It appears that the Iguanodons managed to find land routes all over the world, even traveling from America across Antarctica and into Australia.

# What other animals existed during the Cretaceous period?

Morganucodon was a small early mammal.

**M**AMMALS AND LIZARDS CONTINUED TO LIVE ALONGSIDE THE DINOSAURS, AND snakes began to appear for the first time. The mammals were still small, and the lizards lived in the wet areas of land. The dinosaurs went on dominating Earth right to the end of their existence. No other animals grew so huge or adapted so well to the conditions of the time.

### How had the dinosaurs developed?

The dinosaurs began to live in smaller areas of land separated by seas and oceans. This meant that they couldn't move around as much. Some managed to develop and change, but others couldn't adapt and died out.

New dinosaurs had to evolve to keep up with the changing world. The Tyrannosaurus was one of the last of the new dinosaurs. It was 40 feet long and a meat-eater. It was found in Canada and the USA.

### How were flying animals developing?

Pterosaurs were still ruling the skies, but the first birds had begun to evolve. By the end of the Cretaceous period, there were lots of different birds, very similar to the birds known today. Some of the birds of the time, however, still had teeth.

### Did the first birds develop from the pterosaurs?

Scientists believe that the first bird, Archaeopteryx, was closely related to the dinosaurs. It had many similar features to the reptiles. Although Archaeopteryx was a winged bird, it also had clawed fingers, a bony tail, and even teeth. The first bird may not have been very good at flying, but probably climbed trees and then launched itself into flight from high branches.

### How were the sea creatures developing?

Fish continued to evolve throughout this time. The reptiles that preyed on the fish began to change, resembling the monitor lizards of today. They were called mosasaurs.

Kronosaurus was a reptile that lived in the water and ate fish.

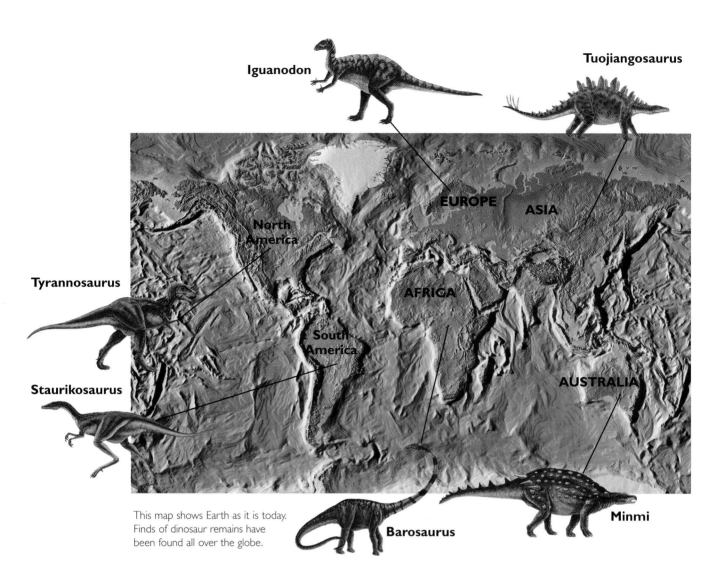

**Iguanodon**

**Tuojiangosaurus**

EUROPE

ASIA

North America

**Tyrannosaurus**

AFRICA

South America

**Staurikosaurus**

AUSTRALIA

This map shows Earth as it is today. Finds of dinosaur remains have been found all over the globe.

**Barosaurus**

**Minmi**

# Where in the world did the dinosaurs live?

DINOSAURS LIVED ON EARTH FOR MILLIONS OF YEARS, AND THEY SAW THEIR PLANET change enormously throughout the three long periods of Earth's history that have already been mentioned. The dinosaurs lived on land, and when they first appeared, at the end of the Triassic period, all the land on Earth was joined together in one piece.

## What was Pangaea?

The earliest dinosaurs lived in a world where all the land was in one place. When they wanted to roam, they didn't need to cross water to travel great distances.

The remains of the earliest dinosaurs have been found in places that are now oceans apart, but in the Triassic period were once part of the same piece of land, known as the Pangaea.

## Were there continents on the Earth?

When the continents began to form and move away from one another, the dinosaurs became isolated. Some of the later dinosaurs have each been found in only one small area because they didn't have great landmasses to walk across.

### Have dinosaurs been found in Great Britain?

There have been some important discoveries of dinosaur bones in Great Britain. 180 years ago a scientist called Gideon Mantell found Megalosaurus bones in Sussex in England. He was one of the earliest paleontologists to study dinosaur bones in Britain.

### Are dinosaur bones still being found in Great Britain?

Dinosaur bones are still being found in Britain, particularly in the Isle of Wight, where some of the first Iguanodon bones were discovered—this island is particularly rich in dinosaur finds.

### What kinds of new dinosaurs are being found?

In China, over the last few years, many new dinosaurs have been discovered, and scientists are still working to find out exactly what they are. The new finds include dinosaurs that were probably covered in feathers.

The Iguanodon has been found on the Isle of Wight.

The Minmi has been found only in Australia.

# Who were the dinosaur collectors?

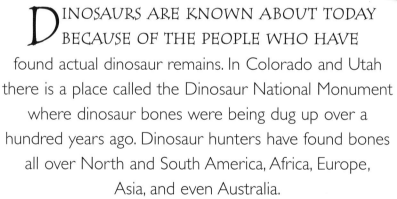

The Dinosaur National Monument, Utah.

DINOSAURS ARE KNOWN ABOUT TODAY BECAUSE OF THE PEOPLE WHO HAVE found actual dinosaur remains. In Colorado and Utah there is a place called the Dinosaur National Monument where dinosaur bones were being dug up over a hundred years ago. Dinosaur hunters have found bones all over North and South America, Africa, Europe, Asia, and even Australia.

### Did the same kinds of dinosaur live all over the world?

Similar types of early dinosaurs have been found all over the world. The later dinosaurs, which were isolated in smaller areas of land, are found in fewer places.

Although the Tyrannosaurus and Tarbosaurus must have been related, they evolved differently because they lived on opposite sides of the world.

17

# What did the dinosaurs eat?

The Struthiomimus was an omnivore.

**M**OST DINOSAURS WERE EITHER MEAT-EATERS OR PLANT-EATERS. Meat-eaters are called carnivores and plant-eaters are called herbivores, and nearly all dinosaurs were either one or the other. There were, however, some omnivores—animals that ate both plants and meat. The Struthiomimus was one of these. It looked something like an ostrich, and ate plants as well as insects and lizards.

The meat-eating Tyrannosaurus would attack other dinosaurs for food.

### What did meat-eating dinosaurs look like?

Meat-eating dinosaurs walked on their back legs, and were strong and fast. They had short necks and large heads with powerful jaws, making it easier for them to catch and kill their food.

Meat-eaters came in all sizes. The Compsognathus was small, less than three feet long. It was very fast with sharp teeth. The most famous dinosaurs are the big meat-eating dinosaurs which grew to over 30 feet long.

### What did plant-eaters look like?

The largest plant-eating dinosaurs—the sauropods—walked on four legs and were the biggest of all. They could grow to more than 100 feet long. They had small heads and long necks, which meant they could reach food high up in trees. Smaller plant-eaters like the Lesothosaurus could walk or run on two legs. This dinosaur grew to between three and six feet and grazed near the ground.

### How did the meat-eaters catch their food?

There were many different meat-eating dinosaurs, but some were very specialized. The Oviraptor, for example, may have eaten eggs, which it scooped up in its three-fingered claws and broke open with its strong jaws.

### What was the largest meat-eating dinosaur?

Before Tyrannosaurus the Allosaurus was the largest meat-eater. It was 35 feet long. Like the later Tyrannosaurus, it had adapted to attacking smaller dinosaurs. It was very strong and could judge distances very well.

The Oviraptor probably ate eggs.

# How did the plant-eaters feed?

THE LARGEST OF THE HERBIVORE DINOSAURS MUST HAVE SPENT ALMOST ALL THEIR TIME eating. They had to eat an enormous amount of food to become so huge. The Diplodocus was 90 feet long, with a long neck to feed from high branches and a very long tail. The large plant-eating dinosaurs had to walk on four feet because of their huge stomachs.

### What kinds of animals did the meat-eating dinosaurs feed on?

The largest meat-eating dinosaurs would prey on other dinosaurs, hunting and killing them. Smaller meat-eaters, however, could not possibly attack bigger dinosaurs, so they would feed on insects, lizards, and the few small mammals that were on Earth at that time. Many of these mammals were not much bigger than mice and could easily be caught and eaten by the smaller meat-eating dinosaurs.

### How did the smaller plant-eaters feed?

Some of the herbivores could be as small as a cat and so couldn't reach high into trees to feed. At this time, the Earth was covered in low-growing plants like ferns, so the smaller plant-eating dinosaurs had plenty to eat at ground level.

### What kinds of plants did dinosaurs eat?

For most of the time the dinosaurs were alive, there were no flowering plants. Most of the plants were like our modern conifers, with leaves shaped like needles, and grew all year round. There were also smaller plants like ferns and horsetails— plants that can still be seen today. Many of the plants had hard, waxy leaves.

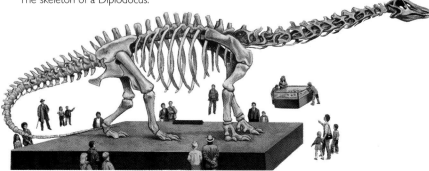

The skeleton of a Diplodocus.

# Were they warm-blooded or cold-blooded?

COLD-BLOODED ANIMALS CANNOT KEEP THEIR BODIES WARM WITH ENERGY FROM FOOD. They are warmed by the sun and get cold when it is dark. Warm-blooded animals keep their body at one temperature all the time. They do this by using the energy from their food to keep them warm.

At ten feet long, the Komodo dragon is the largest modern lizard.

### Were dinosaurs cold-blooded?
Scientists thought that dinosaurs were like reptiles, so they thought they also must have been cold-blooded. Scientists have been looking at the evidence again, however, and are no longer sure that this is true.

### What does it mean to be cold-blooded?
Modern reptiles are cold-blooded. When they become cold, these animals slow down, which can happen at night or during the colder seasons of the year. When a cold-blooded animal cannot move quickly, he is in danger from predators. But dinosaurs do not appear to have slowed down the way modern lizards do, since many of them were hunters and had to be able to move quickly.

Plant-eaters like the Lufengosaurus must have eaten a huge amount of food if they were cold-blooded.

### Were some of the dinosaurs cold-blooded?

Scientists don't know if the largest plant-eating animals were warm- or cold-blooded. Warm-blooded animals need to eat more than cold-blooded ones to keep themselves warm. If these huge dinosaurs were warm-blooded, they would have had to eat a massive amount of food to keep their bodies warm, so they may have been cold-blooded.

### Were some dinosaurs warm-blooded?

Some scientists believe that the long-necked dinosaurs must have been warm-blooded. If they were cold-blooded, these dinosaurs would not have had a high enough blood pressure for blood to reach their brains.

### Is there any other evidence to show whether dinosaurs were warm- or cold-blooded?

The bony plates on some dinosaurs' backs might have evolved to trap the sun's heat and warm their bodies. These dinosaurs were possibly cold-blooded.

The plates on the back of the Tuojiangosaurus may have helped him keep warm if he was cold-blooded.

# What does the evidence show?

THERE IS SOME EVIDENCE THAT DINOSAURS MIGHT HAVE BEEN COLD-BLOODED AND some evidence that they might have been warm-blooded. Nobody knows for certain. There were probably examples of both kinds.

### Will we ever know whether dinosaurs were warm- or cold-blooded?

Scientists are still working to find out more about dinosaurs — what they looked like, and whether they were warm- or cold-blooded. New discoveries are being made all the time, and new dinosaurs are being found. As more and more evidence is gathered, there is a greater chance of finding out just what these creatures were like. Perhaps one day we will know all the answers.

# Did dinosaurs live in herds?

SCIENTISTS HAVE LOOKED AT FOOTPRINTS MADE BY DINOSAURS MILLIONS OF YEARS AGO. These fossils show that some dinosaurs moved around in herds. They lived in groups, sometimes of a hundred or more animals. They traveled and lived together. Some of them even hunted in packs.

### How do we know which dinosaurs lived in herds?

The Apatosaurus was one of the largest plant-eating dinosaurs that lived in herds. This is known because the Apatosaurus' fossilized footprints found in North America were all made at the same time.

The huge Apatosaurus could probably walk at about the speed of a modern elephant—about 15 miles an hour.

### What were the advantages of living in a herd?

The dinosaurs that lived in herds were often plant-eaters, and some of them would have been in danger from meat-eating dinosaurs. So it was probably safer for these dinosaurs to live in groups. Some dinosaur tracks have smaller footprints in the middle of the pack. This shows that the smaller and younger dinosaurs walked in the middle of the herd, protected by the larger, adult dinosaurs around them.

### Did dinosaur herds travel?

Dinosaurs could move very freely around the Earth while all the landmasses were still joined together. Dinosaur herds had to travel to find food because if they always fed in one place, the food would soon become scarce. So they traveled around, sometimes long distances, to find new sources of food.

This photograph shows dinosaur footprints found in Queensland, Australia.

# What kinds of dinosaurs lived in herds?

MOST OF THE HERDING DINOSAURS WERE HERBIVORES, INCLUDING THE LARGE sauropods. The horned dinosaurs, the ceratopsians and the duck-billed dinosaurs, are also thought to have lived in herds, so that they could graze safely. Predators would have found it more difficult to hunt them if they lived in groups.

### What kinds of dinosaurs lived alone?

Meat-eating dinosaurs were more likely to live alone. They had to be able to move fast to catch their food, and this would have been difficult in a herd. Deinonychus was a meat-eating dinosaur that may have hunted in small packs, but would never have formed part of a large herd like the plant-eaters.

### Did the balloons and crests on dinosaurs' heads have a purpose?

Some dinosaurs had crests and balloons on their heads. Scientists think that these may have been used like amplifiers, to make the dinosaurs' noises louder. This would help the dinosaur warn other members of its herd of dangers.

The Parasaurolophus and Saurolophus were dinosaurs that had crests on their heads.

The name Triceratops means "three-horned face" because of the dinosaur's head armor.

# What were the plates and crests?

MANY DINOSAURS HAD ALL KINDS OF ADORNMENTS TO THEIR HEADS AND bodies, including plates, spines, helmets, crests, horns, and spikes. Some of these were hard and bony, others were hollow and fairly fragile, but they must all have evolved for a reason. Scientists have come up with a number of different ideas why dinosaurs might have developed these extra body parts.

**Did the dinosaurs have armor?**

The large meat-eating dinosaurs would eat other dinosaurs that were smaller or badly protected. So many of the slower-moving plant-eaters grew armor to protect themselves. Some grew protection on their heads and some on their bodies or tails as a form of defense.

**How was head armor used?**

Dinosaurs like Triceratops and Styracosaurus had armored heads, with horns and spikes on them. The horns on the heads of these dinosaurs were used for self-defense. Scientists now think that the Triceratops probably also fought one another.

The Pachycephalosaurus had a very hard head.

**Were there other types of head armor?**

The Pachycephalosaurus had a large, thick, domed skull that was a form of head armor. It could head-butt anything that might attack it.

### How was body armor used?

Other dinosaurs had body protection. The Edmontonia from the Cretaceous period was a plant-eating dinosaur that walked on all fours. Its body was covered in plates of defensive armor and its skull was thick. The Edmontonia would have been too slow to get away from a predator, so its armor would help it survive an attack.

The Edmontonia was slow but well protected.

# How were plates used?

STEGOSAURUS HAD PLATES ALONG ITS BACK. IT WAS THOUGHT AT ONE TIME THAT THESE were a form of armor, but new evidence shows that this was unlikely. The hard spikes and horns seen on other dinosaurs probably were armor, but the plates on a Stegosaurus were different. For one thing, they were not well placed for defense. And they were not very deeply rooted in the body, so they would fall off before they could do any damage to another dinosaur. Scientists now believe that these plates may have been used like solar panels to keep the dinosaur's body warm.

### Did dinosaurs use weapons?

Some of the dinosaurs didn't just have defensive armor. The Euoplocephalus had bony spines all over its back, but it also had a clubbed tail to use as a weapon.

The Euoplocephalus could swing its tail to attack.

The Stegosaurus was a plant-eater about 23 feet long.

### Were there other reasons why dinosaurs had these adornments?

Some dinosaurs like Lambeosaurus or Corythosaurus had strange crests on their heads. These are too fragile to have been any use as defense or for head-butting. They may simply have been ornaments to attract other dinosaurs for mating.

# How did dinosaurs reproduce?

DINOSAURS HAVE MORE IN COMMON WITH REPTILES THAN any other modern animals, so it is not surprising that they reproduced in a similar way to reptiles. Female dinosaurs laid eggs, which had leathery shells for protection. Some dinosaurs made nests in the mud in the way that modern crocodiles do.

The Protoceratops probably protected its young.

### What did the eggs look like?

It is nearly 80 years since the first dinosaur eggs were found in the Gobi desert in Mongolia. They looked very much like ordinary eggs. The eggs of some dinosaurs were round and others were oval, like modern birds' eggs. Surprisingly, the eggs were not as big as you might think. The biggest ones found are only about 12 inches long, which seems small when you remember how big some of the dinosaurs were.

### Did male and female dinosaurs look different?

In many species of modern animals the males and females look slightly different. No one is really sure if the same is true for dinosaurs. Scientists have found two slightly different types of the same dinosaur and think these may have been the male and female. It is possible, of course, that males and females were different in their coloring, but very little is known about what color they were. They could have been any color at all.

### How did scientists find out about dinosaur reproduction?

Scientists have found fossils of eggs and nests and even of hatchlings, so they know this is how the dinosaurs reproduced. Although many single nests have been found, some were close together, in groups.

### Did herding dinosaurs nest together?

The giant sauropods, who lived in herds, also nested in herds, creating a nursery. The titanosaurs dug shallow nests in sand—groups of these nests have been found in India.

### How did dinosaurs make nests?

Some of the dinosaur nests were probably just trampled or scooped-out areas of soil or sand, which would have been easy to make. Nests were sometimes also covered, and dinosaurs may have used their smaller front legs to move soil or sand, or gather and spread plants, to achieve this.

# Did dinosaurs take care of their young?

SINCE DINOSAUR EGGS WERE SO SMALL, DINOSAUR BABIES MUST HAVE BEEN VERY small, too. They probably needed care for some time until they grew up and could look after themselves. For example, dinosaur parents may have helped their young feed. And dinosaur footprints have been found which make it clear that smaller dinosaurs traveled along with the adults and may have been cared for by the herd.

**Were dinosaurs good parents?**
Scientists believe that the Maiasaura dinosaur was a very good mother. The word Maiasaura itself means "good mother lizard." This dinosaur built large mud nests and laid about twenty eggs no more than eight inches long. The eggs were then covered to protect them and keep them warm.

Maiasaura took very good care of her eggs and young.

# When did the dinosaur age end?

THE DINOSAURS DIED OUT COMPLETELY ABOUT 65 MILLION YEARS AGO, BUT NOBODY really knows why. The dinosaurs had been the most successful land animals in the world for about 165 million years, but suddenly their age on Earth ended. Dinosaurs did not die out gradually over a long period of time, in the way other animals have, and they do not seem to have evolved into any of the animals we see today. Scientists have been trying for a long time to find out why the dinosaurs suddenly became extinct.

Saltasaurus was one of the last known dinosaurs.

Earth may have been covered in dust and smoke when the dinosaurs became extinct.

## How much had the Earth changed during the dinosaur age?

During the long age of the dinosaurs, Earth changed a great deal. The land split into continents, with oceans and seas between them. The climate changed, bringing more rain and more tropical areas. Vegetation evolved, too, so that instead of just conifers and ferns, flowering plants began to grow. The years also began to have seasons for the first time.

## Why did the dinosaurs become extinct?

The dinosaurs may have simply died out. It may have been partly because they could not evolve fast enough to keep up with the changing world. Throughout the Triassic, Jurassic, and Cretaceous periods, dinosaurs evolved into new kinds of dinosaurs. Some also became extinct. It is, however, strange that all the dinosaurs should have died out at the same time.

## Was there a disaster?

There may have been some kind of disaster at the end of the Cretaceous period, which caused the dinosaurs to die out. This is called an extinction event. There could have been many reasons for a disaster to occur on the Earth at this time. For example, a huge rock from outer space could have hit the planet very hard. That rock might have been a meteor, a comet, or an asteroid, and may have made a vast crater on the planet, causing a huge amount of dust to be thrown out into the Earth's atmosphere. This might have been followed by widespread fires across the globe.

# What happens to the Earth during an extinction event?

IF A CATASTROPHE DID HAPPEN AND THE EARTH WAS COVERED IN DUST AND SMOKE for a long time, this would have blocked out the sun. And without the sun to warm the Earth, plants would have died. The plant-eating dinosaurs would have had nothing to eat. When the herbivores died, the meat-eating dinosaurs would have had nothing to eat, and so all of them would soon have become extinct. This is just one possible explanation.

**Did other creatures become extinct at the same time as the dinosaurs?**
All the dinosaurs became extinct at the end of the Cretaceous period, but there were other animals that disappeared at the same time. Reptiles, like the pterosaurs in the skies and the mosasaurs and plesiosaurs in the water, also died off. At the same time, some of the tiniest creatures of the Earth and seas also disappeared.

**Did any of these creatures have anything in common with dinosaurs?**
All the animals that became extinct at the same time had one thing in common with the dinosaurs. Dinosaurs needed a warm environment that didn't change very much, and the other animals that died out also had to have this kind of climate. Knowing this, scientists are fairly sure that the climate must have changed dramatically to cause the extinction of so many different kinds of creatures.

**What might have happened if the dinosaurs had not died out?**
No one will ever know for sure what would have happened if the dinosaurs had survived. Man is a mammal, and it was not until after the dinosaurs became extinct and the Earth had changed that man began to evolve. Some scientists think that the small mammals, like mice, that lived during the age of the dinosaurs, would never have changed, and that man would never have existed.

# What is paleontology?

WHEN THE FIRST DINOSAUR BONES WERE FOUND ABOUT TWO HUNDRED YEARS AGO, no one had any idea what the animals might have been or when they had lived. Scientists began to study them. People who discover and study fossils are called paleontologists. For the last 140 years they have been trying to find out as much as they can about creatures who lived on Earth a long time ago, including, of course, dinosaurs.

### Who were the first paleontologists?

It was only about two hundred years ago that dinosaurs were recognized as extinct reptiles of some kind. In 1841 a man called Sir Richard Owen first gave them the name dinosaurs.

Sir Richard Owen

The process of fossilization takes millions of years.

### How were the different dinosaurs named?

Once dinosaurs were understood to be an important group of animals, as each different dinosaur was discovered, it was given its own name. These names sometimes look very difficult to say and all of them come from Latin words. They usually describe something special about a particular dinosaur's appearance or habits — for example, Euoplocephalus means "well-armored head."

### How are fossils made?

A fossil is made when an animal dies and is buried in mud. Over a very long time the mud hardens and more mud is layered on top. Eventually it hardens into rock. Then, over millions of years, the rock is gradually worn away again, revealing fossilized bones.

# How are dinosaurs reconstructed?

SOMETIMES SCIENTISTS FIND ONLY A FEW BONES, AND SOMETIMES THEY FIND WHOLE skeletons. Whatever they find, they always keep a careful record of how and where the bones were discovered. They take photographs and keep lists of everything. Then, when they have enough pieces of the puzzle, they are able to reconstruct whole dinosaurs or parts of dinosaurs and identify them. Scientists will often work together and can learn a great deal from the original notes made at dinosaur sites.

Paleontologists work slowly and carefully, making detailed notes of their finds.

### Who collected dinosaur bones?

People have been fascinated by dinosaurs and the science of paleontology for over a hundred years. In Utah, two men named Edward Cope and Othniel Marsh were largely responsible for one of the greatest dinosaur finds ever. They found dozens of huge dinosaur bones in what is now the Dinosaur National Monument.

In 1811 the first female paleontologist, called Mary Anning, began work in Lyme Regis in England.

Edward Cope and Othniel Marsh made one of the greatest dinosaur finds in history.

### What was paleontology like 150 years ago?

The earliest paleontologists simply collected the bones that they found or dug up, and tried to figure out what they could be.

When a bone or part of a dinosaur turned up that had not been seen before, they would name it and try to determine what the animal must have looked like.

Gradually, over time, these early paleontologists began to fit the pieces of the puzzle together.

### What is modern paleontology like?

Modern paleontology is much slower and more painstaking than it used to be. It is no longer simply a matter of collecting old fossils and bones. Modern paleontologists take great care to preserve their finds and record them so that the information can be shared.

Everything we know about dinosaurs has come from more than 150 years of studying bones and fossils. Some paleontologists have even gone back to old sites where bones have been found in the past, just in case the earlier scientists missed anything that a modern paleontologist might find of value.

### What is the future of paleontology?

Thousands of dinosaur bones have been found and collected over the last 150 years. However, if the dinosaurs really did rule the world—and there were no other large animals in existence at that time—there must still be thousands of dinosaur bones that have not yet been discovered. There may even be hundreds of different kinds of dinosaurs that no one knows about.

The study of dinosaurs is likely to go on for a great many years to come, but in the end, maybe some of the big questions about them will be answered at last.

# Index